By the River
of No Return

By the River of No Return

Don Ian Smith

Illustrated by David Dawson

ABINGDON PRESS

Nashville and New York

BY THE RIVER OF NO RETURN

Copyright © 1967 by Abingdon Press

All rights in this book are reserved.

No part of the book may be reproduced in any manner whatsoever without written permission of the publishers except brief quotations embodied in critical articles or reviews. For information address Abingdon Press, Nashville, Tennessee.

ISBN 0-687-04474-X Large-print edition

Library of Congress Catalog Card Number: 67-14991

Scripture quotations unless otherwise noted are from the Revised Standard Version of the Bible, copyrighted 1946 and 1952 by the Division of Christian Education, National Council of Churches, and are used by permission.

The poem, "Memory," which appears on pp. 80-81, is taken from *The Complete Poems of Thomas Bailey Aldrich* (Boston: Houghton Mifflin Company, 1907), and is used by permission.

"Satellites and Saddle Horses" is reprinted from *Together;* copyright © 1967 The Methodist Publishing House. "The Grass Is Greener" and "Have You Heard Any Angels Singing Lately?" are reprinted by permission of *Church Management.*

MANUFACTURED BY THE PARTHENON PRESS AT NASHVILLE, TENNESSEE, UNITED STATES OF AMERICA

To my wife, Betty, whose ability to see and appreciate beauty adds a very special quality to the beauty of Sky Range Ranch

Preface

This little book comes out of many happy years at Sky Range Ranch, our home in the mountains of central Idaho. Sky Range Ranch is situated in the valley of a small tributary of the famed Salmon River, better known as "the River of No Return." This wonderful, wild river cuts the state of Idaho in two with a canyon deeper than the Grand Canyon of the Colorado. It flows through a wilderness where there are no roads, and a boat trip down the river is not only a thrilling adventure, but always a one-way trip. This one-way trip down the River of No Return is to me a symbol of life, for life is always a one-way trip. There can be no going back, but the future is always a challenge and a promise.

Though Sky Range Ranch is home and ranching is my favorite sideline, my real vocation has been that of a country preacher, with some time spent as a probation and parole officer, and some time spent as a teacher. I like to think of myself as a country preacher, but I am sure that my experience as a rancher has given me some valuable insight into the meaning of the word "pastor." My hobbies of hunting and fishing, which take me far from the traveled roads back into the wilderness, where one travels only on steep and winding trails, have given me a chance to know and appreciate country where nature is unspoiled by the demands of civilization.

I know that my love of the country has influenced my theology. I am not ashamed of this. In the city it is easy to become so concerned with the wonders and problems of man that you begin to think that man is the measure of things—perhaps the Supreme Being. In a country of towering mountains and roaring rivers where one lives close enough to nature to note and depend on the changing seasons, it is easy to remember that God alone is great. It is easy to reflect on the wonder of a gospel that tells us that the God of creation is also the God of salvation; the God who put the mountains on their foundations and the rivers in their beds is also one who will feed his flock like a shepherd, and carry the young lambs in his arms.

In the spring, when the new grass comes on the mountains and the little whiteface calves are frolicking after their mothers on the way to summer range, when the wild flowers turn our hills into a million-acre flower garden and the birds come back to the willows along the creek, I feel confident that somehow, in these things of earth, God is giving us an insight into the truth of heaven.

I am a conservationist. My great delight has been the improvement of my little ranch. But I know this is a sideline, and not my real vocation. The task of the country preacher is the same as the task of any preacher—to be a good theologian. I have an interest in soil erosion, but I do not think this is nearly as much my concern as the soul erosion that is going on in our materialistic culture. I know that even in the most beautiful mountains it is quite possible to worship the creation and forget the Creator. I receive great pleasure from conservation measures that improve my land and help me dream of a time when my grandchildren might look upon this land and find it even better than I found it. But as I watch the water trickle down the hills in the spring runoff, I have reason to reflect on the fact that long after I am gone, grass roots will still be making topsoil out of granite. Man passes, but the earth remains. And what does it profit a man if he does contour plowing, uses good fertilizer, has the best system of crop rotation, raises the best cattle, eats well and dresses well, and, in fact, gains the whole world, and loses his soul?

Our life at Sky Range Ranch is a good life. My wife Betty and our children Heather, Rockwell, and Heidi all live active lives in the church and community, but we find time to "moonlight" and tend our cattle—riding range, feeding, irrigating, fixing fence, branding, doctoring. Our children have learned to ride horses as naturally as most children learn to walk.

Our home is surrounded with natural beauty. To the west, the magnificent Lemhi Range rises to 11,000 feet. To the east, we look across the valley of the Lemhi River to the beautiful Beaverhead Mountains that form the Continental Divide and the boundary between Montana and Idaho. The crystal-clear creek that waters Sky Range Ranch has sources hidden high in the hills, and in the hottest days of summer it never fails. It speaks of the unfailing "water of life." Whenever we "lift up our eyes," we know the confidence that welled up in the heart of the psalmist who wrote·

"As the mountains are round about Jerusalem,
    so the Lord is round about his people,
        from this time forth and for evermore" (Ps. 125).

DON IAN SMITH

Contents

By the River of No Return 13
Satellites and Saddle Horses 20
Raspberries by an Irrigation Ditch 26
Symbol on the Steeple 32
Snow in the High Country 36
Scene from a City Dump 41
Have You Heard Any Angels Singing Lately?.. 45
The Fullness of Time 52
Hills and Valleys 58
He Makes Me Lie Down 64
When the Signs Have Been Destroyed 70
Yellow Bells 77
A Guide or a Map 82
With Wings like Eagles 87
The Price of Potatoes 90
The Grass Is Greener 96
Small Talk 102
Like a Shepherd 107

By the River of No Return

"Then he showed me the river of the water of life, bright as crystal, flowing from the throne of God."   Revelation 22:1

To one who enjoys the out-of-doors, one of the greatest experiences possible is a trip on the Salmon River, Idaho's famed "River of No Return" that runs from east to west across the state of Idaho through a wilderness where there are no roads. This river runs through a canyon, part of the deepest canyon system in the United States, a canyon deeper than the better-known Grand Canyon of the Colorado. This river runs so fast and through such a wilderness, you know when you start the trip that you are going all the way, no matter what! There can be no turning back. So for several days you ride the rapids, trusting completely in your boat and your guide, knowing that if these fail, all is lost; yet knowing with a certain sense of joy and wonder that the boat and the guide are trustworthy, and you can have a wonderful trip, and there is no need of ever turning back.

For me, the River of No Return has become a symbol of life. Yesterday is always gone forever, a part of the river we have already run. Tomorrow is always unknown, a part of the river that lies ahead, around a bend, hidden by the towering walls of the canyon. But we do not fear. With confidence in a God who is trustworthy and guides us, carried by a faith that sustains us and our fellow believers in the church, we find a sense of joy and wonder as we make the trip, knowing that we would not go back if we could, and looking always ahead to that which God has prepared for them that love him.

As one watches a boat slip away from the dock at Salmon to begin the long journey (usually about ten days) down the river, he is gripped by the seriousness of a journey on which there can be no going back; a journey on which the only hope lies in pressing onward toward the goal of a safe passage. Often, as I see a little child in the nursery at the hospital, a baby who has just started the journey of life, I am gripped by the same feeling. Surely his only hope lies in making a safe passage on a river which permits no going back. The human spirit must be ever pressing forward for something better tomorrow; always seeking the joy, wonder, and excitement of a one-way trip through fascinating country.

My first introduction to the Salmon River wilderness came when I was a very small boy. I sat with my mouth open as an old mountain man told me tall tales of that wonderful part of the world. One of the stories that will always live in my memory was the story of a mountain sheep, one of those amazingly agile creatures that are native to the crags and peaks of the Salmon River country. The old man told me that one day he was watching this bighorn ram when it decided to cross a great chasm, at least fifty feet wide. The chasm was deep—one slip would mean certain death for the ram. So this mighty ram studied the chasm carefully. Then he backed away about fifty yards, made a terrific run, and a great, arching leap out over the yawning abyss. He was almost to the other side when he realized he couldn't quite make it, so he turned around and went back!

We smile when we picture in our minds that great ram turning around in midair. Yet how often we try to do that very thing in life. We forget that life is a river of no return, and we try to live as if we could go back. We spend hours yearning for "good old days" that can never come again. We talk about returning to normalcy, when there is nothing normal in life, when there is only past and future. A past that cannot be relived; a future that cannot be known.

Jesus was thinking of this when he said: "He who puts his hand to the plow and looks back is not fit for the kingdom." It is his way of saying that we cannot drive safely in life by watching the rearview mirror. The story of Lot's wife points out this same truth. When the future was calling her, she kept looking back to the past, and she turned into the most lifeless, useless thing one can imagine—a pillar of salt in a thirsty, parched desert (Genesis 19:26).

We cannot go back to a prewar world. We cannot go back to a world in which there are no atom bombs. We cannot go back to a world where racial inequality is taken for granted. We cannot go back to a world where we can live with disregard for what goes on at the other side of the world. But we can press on, with the living God as our helper in facing problems and overcoming them. We cannot go back to the "good old days." We can live with a faith that will make good the days that are ahead.

Life is a river of no return. Its sources are hidden high in the mountains of memory. Its destiny is always a far-off tomorrow, by some distant sea where we have never been and from which we will never return. The little streams of pure, clear water high in the mountains remind us of the innocent joys of childhood. Where the brook plays with the rocks and grasses, seemingly unaware of the great forces that will grasp it farther down its course, it is like a child. Then we see the larger river, like the beginning of adult life, when each one of us is slowly realizing his power and his problems. Sometimes there are quiet places along the river, moments of meditation, moments one wishes could be prolonged forever, when the river slips quietly through a flower-filled mountain meadow, and a deer or elk will pause for a drink beside the still waters. But there is always a restlessness; an eagerness to be on its way. There is really never any stopping for anything. There is a force, more powerful than any other force we know, taking the river on to its destiny; a force that says that once the river has started, there can be no going back.

Fortunate is the man or woman, the church or nation, that has learned that life is a river of no return. There are pessimists in our time who speak of a "post-Christian era," as if there might be something to return to. But as Christians, we should know that though there have been some interesting and exciting things on the upper reaches of the river, with God's guidance, there are greater things ahead downstream. We hear the rapids, we tighten the buckles on our life jackets, and we accept the challenge of the rapids with joy and hope. We see the bend in the river and the steep canyon walls. We cannot see ahead, but we do not look with fear. We look ahead with wonder and anticipation. Like Abraham of old, we lift up our eyes to a distant land and go forth, not knowing the way, but knowing God has promised us the land.

Sometimes we wish we could see into the future; perhaps send a scout down the river ahead of us to tell us what is there. But it is not that way. God says: "Live by faith. I have brought you safely this far and I will be with you always, even to the end of the age." Tomorrow may be the end of the age. One of the reasons why our human schemes are not as important as we think they are is due to this very fact. Maybe just when we have our bigger barns on the drawing boards and the blueprints about ready for the contractor, the Lord will say: "Tonight is the night. Your soul is required of you. Whose will these things be?" Maybe the next bend in the river is the last one, as far as we are concerned, in this life. Or perhaps it is just the beginning of a long stretch of peace and prosperity. We do not know. We cannot know, and in terms of eternity, it really doesn't matter very much as long as we are riding the river with joy and love, confident that we are in his hands. So we move on down the river with the faith of one who said: "Forgetting what lies behind and straining forward to what lies ahead, I press on toward the goal for the prize of the upward call of God in Jesus Christ." With such a faith, we go with gladness down the river, free of worry about tomorrow, free to enjoy the scenery and the excitement and the fellowship of our fellow travelers today. We look toward tomorrow as a child waits for Christmas morning, not knowing what his father has for him, but knowing that because of the father's love, it will be good.

Satellites and Saddle Horses

"For thou, O Lord, hast made me glad by thy work;
at the works of thy hands I sing for joy."

Psalm 92:4

October is my favorite month in the high country of the Salmon River wilderness. The aspen leaves have turned to gold with the first frosts. (My daughter used to call the aspens "money trees" and said that with the number that grew on our ranch we were the richest people in the world.) The patches of aspen gold are splashed against the almost solid green background of the fir and pine forests that cover the slopes of the Salmon River Canyon. Perhaps a few of the peaks will be touched with the white of the first snow of winter—dabs of frosting on a giant cake.

The days are warm, the nights are cold. The bull elk is bugling his challenge, and those of us who enjoy big game hunting find a trip into this wonderland of natural beauty a truly exciting and rewarding experience.

It was in October a few years ago that Sputnik I first orbited the earth. Already it seems that we have always been in the Space Age, but it has really not been long since it began. Some friends with whom I go elk hunting each year were with me, and we were camped on a high ridge along the crest of the Salmon River Canyon when Sputnik made that historic trip. Our camp was about fifteen miles from the river road where we had left our trucks and unloaded our horses and mules to make the trip into our wilderness camp—fifteen miles of steep, beautiful, forest trail, accessible only to one who rides a horse or is an unusually avid hiker.

Most of the world knew about Sputnik a couple of days before we did. We had killed our elk, and with our string of mules heavily loaded with meat and camp gear, we made the fifteen-mile trip back to our trucks in what we thought was excellent time. We were congratulating ourselves on making the fifteen miles in less than four hours. Not bad! And then we heard the news! While we had been in the hills, Sputnik had gone around the world in an hour and a half. What a contrast! The speed of the satellite and the plodding pace of the pack string.

Since that historic October such a short time ago, the Space Age has accelerated with fantastic speed. Each fall as we go hunting, our pack string plods along the trail at about the same speed that the Children of Israel traveled as they headed for the land of Canaan. Many times in the years since the first Sputnik I have had reason to compare the speed of the satellite and the pace of the pack string. And the more I have thought about it, the more I am sure that the Space Age has done nothing at all to change the value of a saddle horse for doing what a saddle horse is best fitted to do. As we ride the forest trails on our saddle horses we see things and sense things that can never be known by one who travels even at the speed of a jet plane, to say nothing of that of a satellite. At the pace of the pack string one can see the land, the trees, the flowers, the tracks of the wild animals. We can see and smell and touch the living earth and be a part of it. We have a chance to know the wonder of being alive as part of a living earth, in a way that we can never do as we fly above it. As we compare the speed of the satellite and the pace of the pack string, we have a good chance to consider the difference between speed and getting somewhere. Those who go around the earth in an hour and a half are just going around in circles; they are back where they started so soon that they hardly know they have been anywhere at all. When we have been riding saddle horses for a few days through the wonderland of a western wilderness, we know we have really been somewhere.

I would not in any way make light of the importance of scientific research or the importance of probing space. I am sure a present-day Christian will do his best to keep up with intellectual developments and scientific findings. As a nation, we must keep up-to-date and know what is going on in the world about us. But let us not confuse speed with progress; let us not equate the making of faster machines with the development of man and the search for meaning in life. It is quite possible to go faster and faster in our machines, and at the same time be going backward in the things of the mind and spirit that are really important in the sight of God. It is surely true of space travel that we will see less and less of more and more, and our modern living is too much like that already. A journey through space is all speed and no scenery. Unless you have something worthwhile to do when you get there, a jet trip from coast to coast is not as valuable as an evening stroll around your own neighborhood.

I have a cousin who works for a large company. He travels all over the continent by air. One day I was saying how much I envied his opportunity to see so much of the world, and his answer surprised me. He said: "About all I have seen is the inside of the airports and the inside of the offices where my company officials work." He is so typical of many in our time who have been almost all over the world, yet have seen almost nothing in the world. With our emphasis on speed, we forget that we only see a thing when we see it with our understanding, when we see it with time to reflect on what it means. I have spent an hour by a mountain trout stream watching a mother grouse feeding her chicks. In that time I could have gone almost around the world, but would I have seen anything more worth seeing? With the growing number of cars, and in the interest of our society being able to function, I know we must have our great freeways. But as our highways improve and our speed increases, we will see less and less of our country unless we make a special effort to see it. Speed can so easily become the enemy of the very thing we are hurrying to find. I am a naturally restless person, wanting to do things quickly, and in hunting pheasants my greatest problem is what a hunter calls "walking over the birds." I have hunted a promising field with no results, only to have a more patient hunter come along behind me and take a couple of fine birds. I went so fast that the birds just sat tight and I never saw them. The same is true in fishing, and I have known the pleasure of taking a fine trout right behind someone who hurried too fast to properly "work the water." Life can become increasingly empty as speed becomes an end in itself.

Next time you find yourself saying, "I've sure got to hurry," ask yourself honestly: Why? It may be you are hurrying right past the thing you want most in life. Imagine yourself standing by the sea of Galilee when a strangely provoking young man walks up to you and says: "I would talk with you awhile." But you say: "Sorry, sir, I am in such a hurry." So you leave him standing there, and you hurry away from the greatest moment of your life.

Raspberries by an Irrigation Ditch

"Be still, and know that I am God."—Psalm 46:10

I remember a wonderful summer morning when the sun was just peeking over the Continental Divide in the east and was coming down the mountain that stands to the west behind Sky Range Ranch.* I was in the upper meadow changing the set in my irrigation ditch, hurrying to get it done before breakfast

---

* The state of Idaho is named for the Shoshoni Indian words *Ee dah how,* which mean, "The sun is coming down the mountain," or, "It is morning." There is a startling beauty about sunrise in the deep valleys. While the valley floor is still dark, the sun catches the snow-capped peaks, and then its rays move rapidly down the mountainside.

26

so I could hurry through breakfast, so I could hurry to my office, so I could "be on time." Suddenly I discovered a wonderful wild raspberry bush growing by the irrigation ditch. I had not seen it before, and it was loaded with ripe wild raspberries. I remember thinking it would be so good if I just had time to sit down and eat those raspberries, but of course I didn't have time.

Then something struck me, almost like a conversion experience. It was as if a voice was speaking to me and it said, if you don't have time to enjoy a lovely thing when you find it—a lovely thing that will soon be gone and cannot wait another day—what is the use of irrigating, and what is the use of having Sky Range Ranch, and what is the use of going to the office, and what is the use of living? So I just took the time to eat those wild raspberries, to enjoy their dew-covered freshness on that morning that was so alive with freshness, beauty, and light that one could be certain that the Creator was still at work in his world.

If life is so rushed that we cannot stop and appreciate a lovely thing, it is too rushed. The goal of life is not some great moment of achievement that will "happen someday." It is appreciation of the many wonderful little moments that we find all along the way, if we have eyes to see and ears to hear. And if we are going so fast that we miss these lovely little moments, we are going fast enough that we will miss life itself. We will be like the man who went to the picnic in his fast new car and drove right past the picnic grounds, never seeing it.

No people has ever been free from the temptation to worship idols. For many of us speed has become an idol; we take pride in doing obeisance to our idol by being in a hurry. The number of people who say they are too busy to worship and really believe it is tragic. If you feel you are in a hurry and life is pushing you too fast, try this checklist. If you are too busy for these things, you are too busy:

(1) Are you too busy to go to church and to discuss with your family the topic of the sermon?

(2) Are you too busy to sit down from time to time with your husband or wife, without the pressure of a schedule, and talk over your hopes and dreams as you did when you were going together before you were married?

(3) Are you too busy to spend some time with your children doing what they want to do, not what you want to do?

(4) Are you too busy to do some reading of something that is of more lasting significance than the newspaper or a news magazine?

(5) Are you too busy to pray?

(6) Are you too busy to appreciate beauty in the world about you?

I remember a good friend of mine who lay very near death for several days. He was so weak he could not read, or talk, or have anyone talk to him. But he found a great help and comfort in thinking through the words of the great hymns and scriptures that he had committed to memory earlier in his life. It is frightening to me to think of the number of us today who, in this situation, would have no store of great words to think on. We have been in such a hurry that we have never had time to commit to memory any great passages of literature. Many couples who have problems in their homes could solve the problems if they simply took time to think and talk together without hurry. The number of children who grow up without ever having their parents take time for serious conversation with them is amazing.

As we work with the teen-age members of our society, we hear two statements that are so opposite it would be amusing if it were not so sad. One moment they will say, "There isn't a thing to do around this town," and then when you have proposed an interesting project they will say, "We just haven't got time." This odd dilemma comes from the fact that with our emphasis on hurry, we don't know how to get into anything deeply enough to find out that it is really interesting. Like the tiger that paces back and forth in his cage at the zoo, we are in a hurry with nothing to do; speeding, with time on our hands.

We find this same thing in our organizations; people hurrying to get to committee meetings without ever questioning the value of what the committee is doing. Like a squirrel in a treadmill, we run because it turns and it turns because we run, and we never take time to figure out that if we would stop running, some of our pointless meetings would stop meeting and we might have time to read a psalm, or look at a flower, or say a prayer.

With speed an end in itself, we miss knowing people. Some time ago I flew by jet from New York City to Salt Lake City. I barely had time to talk with the man across the aisle; I cannot say I got to know him. A few years earlier I made the same trip by train and came away knowing several people well enough to exchange Christmas cards for a year or two. But three generations ago when my great-grandparents made this trip by covered wagon, those with whom they traveled became lifelong friends. I would not carry this too far. I don't want to return to the covered wagon. But we must remember that speed is not an unmixed blessing and it can rob us of the best things in life if we are not careful how we use it.

In the rush of modern living we need to see the

difference between speed and getting somewhere. In our Space Age with its emphasis on speed and distance it is good to remember that the one who made the greatest impression on the history of the world, the one in whose life we find our life, is one who never traveled faster than a man or donkey can walk, and who never got much farther than one hundred miles from the place where he was born.

Symbol on the Steeple

The Methodist Church in Salmon, Idaho, has a tall, slender steeple. As you approach the church from the south, the Beaverhead Mountains, which form the Continental Divide and the boundary between Montana and Idaho, provide a scenic background; and sometimes, when the sky is just right, it looks as though the cross on the steeple of the church is standing right on top of the mountain range. What a thought—the cross of Christ right on top of the continent!

I remember walking to the church one morning when a light wind was blowing, and I wondered what sort of weather the wind would bring. I looked up at the steeple and I thought, if there was a weather vane on the steeple, I would know which way the wind is blowing. I went into the church and sat down, and for a while I pondered the idle thought that had come to me; and then I said to myself, thank God that on our steeple there is a cross, and not a weather vane.

How sad it would be if we were to go to church to find out the direction of the wind, whether the wind from the north or the wind of public opinion. It is an easy thing to make a god of public opinion; and if we worshiped public opinion, a weather vane would be a proper symbol to put on our churches, and the public opinion poll or survey would be a proper way to seek the favor of such a god.

When we are tempted to bow the knee to the god of majority opinion, it is good to look back across the pages of history and see how often the majority has been wrong. In our Christian history this has been almost a definite rule.

Moses did not have a majority with him when he came down from Sinai, nor did he ask for the ratification of the Commandments before giving them to the people. Elijah certainly did not have a majority behind him on Mt. Carmel when he faced the angry people and cried out: "Why do you go limping with two different opinions? If the Lord is God, follow Him."

When Amos came down from his sheep camp in the hills of Tekoa to speak to the city people in Bethel, he did not carry a book of statistics under his arm. He did not stop to ask by the way: "What are the popular opinions in the city concerning the future of our land, and what would the people like to hear me say to them?" But as one who carries a great message from his superior officer, he cried out:

> Surely the Lord God does nothing,
> > without revealing his secret
> > to his servants the prophets.
> The lion has roared;
> > who will not fear?
> The Lord God has spoken;
> > who can but prophesy?

In a synagogue in Nazareth a man speaks as one having authority, and not as one of the scribes. Where does he get his authority? Has he asked the people? Has he consulted with the bureau of public information? Has he sought the advice of an expert? But no. It is the voice of God himself speaking in the synagogue at Nazareth. And the people are filled with wrath, but it is still the voice of God. And the voice of the people is not the voice of God, even if all the people agreed that it should be.

So I am glad there is a cross on the steeple of our church. I think weather vanes are nice. I like them. I think they belong on barns.

Snow in the High Country

Each year at Sky Range Ranch there comes a morning, usually in late August or early September, when the one in the family who gets up first goes to the window, takes a look at the hills, and shouts: "There's snow in the high country." This is not a cry of sadness, but of joy; yet it has in it a definite declaration that things have changed and summer is past.

The first snow on the mountains is a sight of breathtaking beauty. It is probably just a light dusting of snow; it will melt in the warm autumn sunshine that is still to come. But it makes a sharp contrast to the green and brown and gold of the summer hills, and it tells us that a change of season has begun.

Nights are cool at Sky Range, even in summer, but after the first snow comes on the mountaintops, there is a subtle difference in the coolness of night. Somehow the fire in the fireplace seems just a little more important to the comfort of our home; the extra blanket on the bed at night brings a sense of security it did not bring on chilly summer nights.

Snow in the high country brings other changes. It seems that all summer we are planting things in the garden so there will always be something "coming on." But after that first snow our minds never turn to thoughts of planting, only to thoughts of harvesting. Something in the air seems to say there is a time for planting and a time for taking up what has been planted, and the time for reaping has come. The days of September and October are among the loveliest of the year, yet for some strange reason, though the sun is warm, things do not grow; they seem only to be in haste to ripen, mature, and prepare themselves for winter.

These autumn days are good days. There is a satisfaction and a contentment in them. You look at your hunting rifle as you have not looked at it during the summer, and the thought of elk steak is pleasant, though the hunting trip may still be several weeks away. You look at the apples on your trees; almost overnight they have become ripe and sweet. And the weeds in the garden, a source of annoyance all summer, are no longer a challenge. They are not growing fast now, and you can wait and plow them under instead of pulling them. These autumn days are good with a goodness almost impossible to describe. It is not the sweetness of young love, but the deep, abiding joy of an old love that wears well and has come to be a precious part of you. There is a pleasure in these autumn days that is almost smug; almost you feel like the fat rock chuck who sits in the sun by his den, taking one last long look at the beauty of the earth before he curls up in his warm nest for a happy hibernation.

There are moments in life when you catch a glimpse of snow in the high country. There is that moment when you take your daughter down the aisle to give her away (she was never really yours, but God has let you have her for awhile), and you turn and look at your wife, and you know you are not young anymore. But you know something else: There are things much more important than merely being young. There is that day when you want to ride that salty little colt. You remember other colts you trained, and you know you can handle this one all right, but your grandson says: "Say, Gramp, you'd better let me ride him." And instead of arguing you say: "Sure, Son, top him off for me." And you are proud to see how well the kid rides—but you get a glimpse of snow in the high country.

Spring is a wonderful time—new beginnings, fresh hope, young love, new life. Summer is pure joy—things growing; the earth pouring out her abundance. And blessed is the man who can see snow in the high country and greet it with a shout of expectation, knowing that for everything there is a season and every season has its own reward.

"There is . . . a time to be born, and a time to die; a time to plant, and a time to pluck up what is planted . . . a time to weep and a time to laugh."

Snow in the high country means that the hard work of summer is past; it means the lovely, reward-filled days of autumn are at hand. It also means that the days are getting shorter, and though we have given much time and effort in life to getting things that mean much to us, we will do well to practice the fine art of letting things go without regret.

When the snow comes in the high country we start putting things away for the winter, things like patio furniture and lawn tools. And there is work to be done in the garden. My wife and I are very fond of flowers. We like the bright blooms of our early-blooming annuals. But in the autumn when we prepare the garden for winter, it seems we have a special regard for our perennial plants, those plants that we know will bloom again another springtime.

Scene from a City Dump

The little city of Salmon, Idaho, has the most scenic city dump in the world. At least I think so, and if there is a city that would like to challenge my claim, we can have a "beauty contest" for city dumps. An impartial committee could be appointed to visit each dump and report on the scenery visible from the dump site. Now understand carefully. I am not saying the dump itself is beautiful. I know many cities that have dumps that are in better form. I am speaking now only about the view that can be seen from the site of the dump.

As one stands at the Salmon city dump he can see a great "Y" etched in the earth's crust by two rivers that come together at Salmon. The dump, being on an elevated spot overlooking the junction of the two rivers, provides a fantastic view. One can see for fifty miles up the Lemhi River, a river whose valley is formed by the Lemhi Range on the south and the Beaverhead Range on the east. The valley itself cradles some of the nation's finest cattle ranches, and from the mountains on either side there are over one hundred creeks that rise on the crest zone of the mountains and join the Lemhi River in the valley.

At Salmon, the Lemhi River joins the main Salmon River just a few miles from the place where the Salmon River turns west to start its descent through the canyon that has given it the name, the River of No Return. The Salmon River Canyon is deeper than the famed Grand Canyon of Colorado, and from the Salmon city dump one can look upstream, right up through the great canyon above Salmon. One can look to the north and west downstream through the same canyon, and on to range after range of mountains that form the great Idaho wilderness. This is the scene from the city dump!

But the dump is a dump! Like most city dumps, it is composed of old cars and cans, bottles, radios, mattresses, and bedsteads—all the unpleasant castoffs of our civilization. If one walks about the city dump with his eyes and interests fastened to the things that are in the dump, there is no difference between this dump and any dump. When I have visited this city dump I have often pondered the importance of the phrase: "I lift up my eyes." The scene from the dump is amazing, but it is only for those who lift up their eyes. Unless the eyes are lifted up, one is visiting an ordinary, nasty city dump.

We do not want a religion that is "otherworldly." But there are times when the problems of this world get confusing and we become weary of the routine of life. We need to gain the perspective of the longer look. There is great beauty in the skyline of a city, but I knew a boy who visited a great city and never saw it because he kept his eyes glued to the sidewalk in the hope of finding a dime. The immediate problems of life must be dealt with, but we can see them better and deal with them better if from time to time we see them against the background of the long look that we get when we lift up our eyes.

Long ago a wise man found this source of help. He had his troubles, no doubt. He had to make a living, he needed new furniture, the kids needed shoes, and his home, like every human home, had its misunderstandings and quarrels from time to time. But he found that if he lifted up his eyes beyond the immediate front yard of his house, he could see the everlasting hills. Seeing the hills, he was reminded of

God, reminded that tomorrow is another day, reminded that there is more to life than the solving of the immediate problem that had him temporarily defeated. We cherish his comments in Psalm 121 when he tells us of his experience.

> I lift up my eyes to the hills. . . .
> My help comes from the Lord,
>   who made heaven and earth.

In the story of God's covenant with Abram (Genesis 13), there is a sidelight that is very interesting. God said to Abram, "Lift up your eyes, and look from the place where you are . . . for all the land which you see I will give to you." It is interesting that he had to see it to receive it. Many of the things in life are like that. And many people who think that life is unpleasant or nasty or dull are people who simply will not lift up their eyes. You can visit the Salmon city dump and see only a dump, but you can also lift up your eyes and see one of the most thrilling scenes in all of God's creation.

Have You Heard Any Angels Singing Lately?

Christmas is a wonderful time at Sky Range Ranch. It was on a "silent night" that Christ was born. Silence is a gift of God, and quietness is often his way of speaking. Quietness is one thing that we have in our mountain valley in vast abundance. When we read the Christmas letters that come from our friends telling of their hurried lives, there are times when we wish we could send to our friends, for our Christmas giving, great packages of quietness. The year has come full circle. Our garden, recently filled with flowers, is deep in snow. But beneath the snow there lies the promise of another springtime. From our window we can see the stars that hang low over the snow-covered mountains, and one very bright star just above the mountains to the east we like to call the Star of Hope. So there is promise in the earth; and there is richer promise beyond the earth.

Our neighbor's house is a mile down the valley and around a bend. When our lights are turned off, we see no other man-made lights. Our elevation of 4,700 feet gives us an atmosphere so still and clear that on a winter night it seems that the distance between earth and the stars disappears almost entirely. On Christmas Eve we like to watch these stars and remember that they are the very same stars that shone on the shepherds who watched their flocks by night; they are the very same stars that guided the wise men. And in the eternal light of the stars it is not only the distance between earth and the stars that disappears, but the distance between our home and the manger of Bethlehem.

Of all the Christmas carols that we love to sing, we like best the one written by Phillips Brooks—"O Little Town of Bethlehem." There is no other carol that combines so well the beauty and sentiment of Christmas with the fundamental meaning of Christmas. How better could it be said: In the common life of a dark little town a child is born, and in that birth are the hopes and fears of all the years of his-

HAVE YOU HEARD ANY ANGELS SINGING LATELY?

tory. So silently the gift is given; and even as Christ was born long ago, we pray he may be born in us today. "We hear the Christmas angels, the great glad tidings tell." But do we? Here is the question for us to ponder in these hurried, noisy times in which we live. Have you heard any angels singing lately?

There were angels around when Christ was born. I checked twenty of the most popular Christmas carols and twelve speak of angels. The Bible story of the Nativity certainly does not play down the angels. But what has become of them in our time? Are angels extinct? Could it be that they have gone the way of the dodo bird and the passenger pigeon? Perhaps jets and satellites and all the various radio waves around in space these days have frightened the angels away from the earth. I heard about a device using high-frequency sound to keep pigeons away from a church tower. It works. Perhaps the modern devices breaking the sound barrier have chased the angels away from earth. It's an interesting thought, but angels are not the sort of things to be bothered by jet planes or satellites or high-frequency sound. Perhaps our ability to hear the angels has been affected by the way we live. I knew a man who worked in a boiler factory and lost his ability to hear music. If we haven't heard any angels at Christmastime for several years, perhaps it is time to check up on our way of life and see if we are doing something that is impairing our ability to hear the angels sing.

Our technical advances are wonderful, but with improved technical devices we have lost many fine arts. Very few people today know how to make cloth; the making of good cloth used to be a great source of satisfaction to a good weaver. The art of candlemaking is gone; it is difficult to find anyone who can drive a team of horses; it is even very hard to find a good stonemason. Perhaps the art of angel-listening has gone the same way.

Angel-listening may be something like bird-watching. Bird-watching is coming into popularity now, and as people learn the art of bird-watching they find there are many more birds around than they thought there were. Many people who do not practice the art are completely unaware of the presence of birds. It could be there are angels around that we could hear if we learned how to listen for them. A good bird-watcher learns that he must watch at the right time and in the right place. He will spend hours practicing his art. And there are some places you just don't see birds, no matter how hard you watch.

There are some places you just don't hear angels. You are not likely to hear them at big parties. I won't say you can't, but it is not likely. There were probably some big parties in Bethlehem the night that Christ was born. We know the town was so crowded that there was no room in the inn for Mary and the baby. There is no evidence in the record that any of the partygoers heard any angels that night.

According to the story, who heard the angels? There was Mary. She was a devout young woman expecting her firstborn child. In many ways this must surely be the greatest event in any woman's life. She has shared with God in the act of creation. Her own life will never be the same again, as she shares with her husband in the life of the new little creature that has been created within her.

Mary was wondering about the meaning of all this. She was wondering if she was equal to the great challenge of guiding a new life into the world; she was wondering if she was worthy of the great honor and privilege of being a mother and sharing with God in bringing his child into being. Undoubtedly she had prayed much, and very sincerely, seeking God's guidance. It was in such a mood of reflective, personal, worship that she heard the angels' song. She became aware of the fact that God was speaking to her in a personal way and she replied, saying, "My soul magnifies the Lord." She was listening when she heard the angel.

The shepherds were watching their flocks; they were not watching TV. They were surrounded by the quietness of the hills on a starlit night. The sheep were bedded down and the dogs were asleep by the fire. The conversation among the shepherds had lagged, and they were alone with their thoughts and their prayers. They were devout men who had been looking for a Savior. They were thinking long thoughts. What is the meaning of life, after all? Is it just to work day after day, tending sheep until at last you are too old; and then to live a while longer, a burden to your family and friends; and then to die and rot, and that is all there is to it? Does the God who put the stars in the sky really care about poor shepherds? Does he even care about us as much as we care about our sheep and our good, faithful dogs? "And an angel of the Lord appeared to them, and the glory of the Lord shone around them." And the angel said for them to be not afraid. He had an answer to their questions; he had something to fill the hunger of their hearts.

There are many people who believe they have heard the angels sing. I do not want to seem presumptuous, but I think that I have heard them sing. I have heard them at Christmastime and at other times too. I have heard them sing at weddings, and baptisms, and at the Communion service. I have heard them singing softly at an open grave when a man of faith has quietly committed his lifelong mate into the hands of an all-wise and merciful God.

Angels are our way of describing otherwise indescribable spiritual experiences in which we become aware of some eternal truth that God wants us to know. Angels are our way of describing insights into the very heart of life, those moments when we know God.

Here are some places where you might try listening for angel songs.

As you tuck in a sleeping child on Christmas Eve, think of all God has done for you in giving this child into your care; think of the opportunities in the years ahead to lead this child into the love of God; think of the wonderful thing that has come to pass in your own life and listen carefully. You may hear the angels singing. As you gather your family around your own Christmas tree in your own home and share your gifts with those you love, listen closely. You may hear the angels sing. If you have the good fortune to be able to get away from man-made light for a little while on a clear, starlit night, look up at the heavens and watch the "silent stars go by." Listen! You may hear the angels sing.

The Fullness of Time

February is the month of expectation at Sky Range Ranch. Most of our cows have their calves in March so that the calves will be old enough to turn out on the range when the grass is ready in May, old enough to wean in October or November before winter feeding begins. So we hope for our calves in March, and by good management we get most of them at that time. A late calf means a light calf at weaning time, and a good deal less money for our summer's work.

One of the pleasures of working with cattle is the fact that they are a part of nature. They are not mechanical. Though they are domestic cattle, there is still something of the wild creature about them. One can manage them to a certain extent, but beyond that they will take their own good time about what they do.

Often in February when I go among my cattle, I get impatient for the calves to come. I am eager to know if the calves will be of good quality; if they will be big and healthy. Sometimes I would like to shout at my cows and say: "Hurry up. Produce! Bring forth your calves." But they just chew their cuds contentedly and look at me as if to say, "Relax. In the fullness of time the calves will come and there is nothing you can do to hurry us up." And I know that I might organize a committee or hold a hearing for quicker calves, but still it would not help. In the fullness of time—but no sooner—the calves will come, the snow will melt on the mountain, the grass will come on the hills, and the birds will come back to the willows along the creek.

It is a good thing for a hurried modern man to come up against something he cannot hurry, for so many of the best things in life are like that. If we limit our lives to the things we can control and hurry or retard at will, we limit our lives to things that are very shallow and unimportant. In one of the great teachings of our Lord, he said: "The kingdom of God is as if a man should scatter seed upon the ground, and should sleep and rise night and day, and the seed should sprout and grow, he knows not how. The earth produces of itself, first the blade, then the ear, then the full grain in the ear" (Mark 4:26-28). Our Lord is saying that after the farmer has his crop in the ground and has done his part, he might just as well sleep at night. The outcome of the harvest is in hands much greater than the hands of the farmer; there is not one thing he can do to hurry the grain that will appear "in the fullness of time." Knowing that there are great forces working for him, forces he cannot change, the farmer might as well trust the processes of God and take time to be sociable with his neighbors, kind to his wife, and interested in his children. No amount of watching, worrying, pushing, or pulling will hurry the quiet, ever-active processes of God.

This parable is not just for farmers. How much peace and joy would increase in the world if we would all remember that there are many good things that depend not only upon our efforts but upon the "fullness of time." Modern man has taken so many things into his own hands that he begins to believe that those hands must always be active or the world will stop. We live in a wonderful world, but we cannot enjoy it. We seem to think if we stop to enjoy the world, the world itself might stop. Forgetting that we have a God who "neither slumbers nor sleeps," we think we can neither slumber nor sleep.

Modern man has become so concerned with his part in creation that he can no longer trust what will happen when he isn't there. He can no longer let things happen; he feels he must always make things happen. So life becomes one vast cocktail party where we feel we have failed if we do not keep the conversation moving, if for a few moments there is quietness, with no man saying anything at all. Because he feels that the world depends on him, modern man can no longer live like a lark or a lily. He can neither let down nor let up. And yet he is lonely and afraid. He is like a little boy who has taken his father's big car without permission, and as he drives out on the freeway he knows, deep down in his heart, that it is really too big for him and he does not know enough to drive it safely.

This is a frightening world, and one cannot live in it without faith that he can plant and cultivate, and then leave the harvest in the hands of God. When one hears the newscasts and wonders what the future holds, what a comfort it is to know that in the midst of all man's meanness and cruelty and failure there is another stream of events flowing silently along. God is letting his seeds grow, and he will bring about his purposes "in the fullness of time, we know not how." One of the great passages of the Old Testament is in Genesis 8; after the flood, the promise: "While the earth remains, seedtime and harvest, cold and heat, summer and winter, day and night, shall not cease." God is dependable and his plans are working regardless of what men do.

When my daughter was about four years old, I helped her plant a little garden of her own. She was thrilled with the idea that she could put little gray seeds into the ground and they would grow into beautiful flowers. So she planted her seeds, and then each morning she went out into the garden and dug them up to see if they had grown. And they never did. When we forget God we often live like this; so busy minding God's business that we defeat our own desires.

One day, "in the fullness of time," you will stand on the step of eternity, ready to walk into the glorious presence of the Father. You may pause on the step and look back at the road you have traveled and, looking back, you will wonder why you were ever so anxious and frantic. You will say: "If I had only known when I faced that dread disease; if I had only known when I was so worried about my job; if I had only known in the midst of my despair over the future of mankind; if I had only known how God was working out his purposes and his marvelous design in all of this, how his seed was growing even while men slept; if I had only known, I would not have been so troubled. I would have been more calm, confident, and cheerful. I would have been more loving and much easier to live with."

When we become too wrapped up in the doings of man, it is time to go out on a warm spring night; to look up into the sky and compare the greatest of men's satellites with the great satellite that God has already put in orbit—the one we commonly call the moon. It is time to ponder the mystery of seed that grows even while a man sleeps, and a kingdom that comes "in the fullness of time" as surely as springtime follows winter, grass grows, flowers bloom, and birds build nests and sing, even when we have not shown them how to do it.

Hills and Valleys

The other day I heard a sportscast about a prizefight. The champion won by a decision, and the reporter said: "There were no knockdowns." Most of us, in the battle of life, don't get along that easily. If we really mix it up and live an adventuresome life, we have times when we get knocked flat on our backs. This doesn't mean God is picking on us. It may mean he is trying to show us something and wants us to get a different viewpoint.

When I was a boy we lived in a house that still had that old-fashioned institution called a woodshed. My evening chores included the cutting of kindling. But one day the ax was missing. Someone had misplaced it, and for several days I searched the shed and the yard, trying to find my ax. Then one day I went into the woodshed for some wood and stumbled and fell. I had a nasty fall, and I remained for a few minutes flat on my back, trying to get my breath. Lying there on the floor, looking up, I found my ax. Someone taller than I had put it up on a sill under the eaves, in a place I could never have seen from a standing position. It was a good little ax, and I was glad to have it back. I have remembered that experience and the fact that sometimes we can see things from a worm's-eye view that we cannot see from any other position or point of view. The ups in life are fine. But when the downs come, it is good to know that God is also there and he may be trying to show us something that we have missed when the sun was shining and the weather was good and we were singing "everything's going my way."

Today, with television, many of us get to see the great game of football. But by just watching the games, and generally the ball carrier, we do not see the basic training of a good football player. Certainly one of the most important things that a good player must learn and practice over and over is how to fall down. And not only how to fall down, but how to be knocked down hard and still get up and get back into the game. And in the game of life one of the things we must learn is that we can be knocked down and God is down there on the ground with us. He is not being mean to us; he is just teaching us good fundamentals so we can be better players. He wants us to be able to play the whole game and win in the long run, and we can't expect to do it all standing up.

Much of the pessimism in religion today is because we have not learned to sing, "Sometimes I'm up, sometimes I'm down, O yes, Lord." We think we are supposed to be up all the time, and, like children, we become peevish when we are not.

When we study the lives of truly great Christians, it is interesting to note how many of them really came to know God in the hard places instead of the pleasant places. I have heard people make light of "foxhole" religion. But many men who found that God was in the foxhole with them and were thankful for it have found that God has been more real to them ever since that day he shared the foxhole with them, and their foxhole has become a shrine.

Sometimes a great loss has opened the door for God, sometimes a severe illness. God often uses despair to bring us closer to him, and we must remember that we do not get beyond his reach because we are going through the valley of despair. He is God of the valleys as well as God of the hills.

The story of Ahab's war with Benhadad, the king

HILLS AND VALLEYS

of the Syrians, has some great wisdom in it for our times. Benhadad's troops greatly outnumbered the army that Ahab, king of Israel, could muster. Ahab decided to capitulate. But Benhadad drove his advantage so far and was so unreasonable in his demands that upon the advice of his elders Ahab decided to fight. In a surprise attack, while Benhadad was involved in a drinking party, Ahab's smaller force dealt Benhadad and his Syrians a crushing defeat.

In explaining the defeat, the servants of the king of Syria said to him: "Their gods are gods of the hills, and so they were stronger than we [in the hills]; but let us fight them in the plain, and surely we shall be stronger then they." (I Kings 20:23.) So the following spring Benhadad mustered another large army, as large as the one he had lost, and went again to battle.

The people of Israel encamped before them like two little flocks of goats, but the Syrians filled the country. And a man of God came near and said to the king of Israel, "Thus says the Lord, 'Because the Syrians have said, "The Lord is a god of the hills but he is not a god of the valleys," therefore I will give all this great multitude into your hand and you shall know that I am the Lord.'" (I Kings 20:27-29.)

In other words, you shall know that I am the Lord

of the hills, and the valleys, and everything else. As we would put it today, you shall know that I am the Lord. Period! And the battle was joined again, and again a small force destroyed a much greater force. For Benhadad had made the fatal mistake of underestimating the power of God. He had recklessly gone into the battle on the assumption that God was Lord of the mountains but not of the valleys; that there were places you had to reckon with the Lord and other places where you could ignore him.

There is a great lesson for us in this old story, for many of us are losing battles for the same reason that the king of Syria lost his battle. We are thinking of God as a very limited God. We are thinking that if he is one place, then he is not in another place. If he is in the hills, we will not be concerned with him in the valleys.

Today we meet people who seem to think that God is in church but not in the labor union, or the management conference, or the cocktail party, or the science laboratory, or the weekend picnic. Assuming that God is limited to certain areas of life, we go into other areas of life thinking we are without him; and then we are confused and frustrated, wondering why our plans didn't work out for us, when they could not have possibly worked out because we overlooked the most important aspect of the situation: the fact that

God was there, and we were ignoring his presence.

Because I love the mountains and have spent many wonderful hours in them, I find the old story of Ahab and Benhadad very meaningful for me. Sometimes I have spent a day or two in the mountains and found myself thinking it would be wonderful if I could just stay in the quiet, peaceful, worshipful setting where it is so easy to lift up my eyes and be reminded of the Creator from whence my help comes. I find myself, like Peter, wanting to stay on the Mount of Transfiguration. And then I remember Benhadad, who lost the battle because he thought that God was only in the mountains. I remember that Ahab won the battle because he had confidence that the Lord was Lord of the hills and the valleys, and I am reassured that God will be with me in the work, problems, and successes and failures down in the valley just as surely as he has been with me on the mountain, beside the beautiful creek where I like to make my camp. It is good to be on the mountaintop with the sunshine warm on your back and the world at your feet, but it is sometimes more important to remember that God is also in the shadow of the valley.

He Makes Me Lie Down

"He makes me lie down in green pastures.
He leads me beside still waters;
   he restores my soul."   Psalm 23:2-3

It is very satisfying to give someone something he really wants. One of the pleasures of being a stockman is the pure enjoyment of feeding cattle or sheep when they are hungry; the pleasure of watching these creatures satisfy their need for food; the sense of achievement one feels in having had a part in preparing the food or leading the animals to the pasture where the food is available.

When one turns his cattle onto a green meadow

after they have been brought in from the dry range, it is pure pleasure just to sit your horse awhile and watch. At first the cattle are so excited with the rich new pasture that they run about like children after the sack has been broken at a piñata party and they are scrambling for the goodies. The cows are in such a hurry to eat all the grass that they don't even stop to graze. They just take a bite here and a bite there as they hurry about. Then pretty soon they seem to realize that there is more than enough and they settle down to serious grazing. Biting and swallowing, biting and swallowing, never taking time to chew. This is why a cow has four stomachs; so she can graze in haste and chew in leisure.

When cattle first go on good pasture their grazing has a quality of frenzy about it. Their greed reminds one of people in a bargain basement. Then after a few hours they begin, one by one, to find shady spots along the creek where they will drop down to rest, to spend many hours chewing what they have so hastily gathered. They have come to a time when they simply must stop gathering and lie down. It is at this time of day that I like to ride among my cattle, seeing their contentment, knowing I have cared for them well.

And it is at this time of day that I have pondered the great shepherd psalm. That stockman of long ago, considering his own flock and thinking of the goodness of God, did not say: "He makes me graze in green pastures." Not at all! The wise shepherd put the emphasis somewhere other than on the grazing. He knew that it is even more important to lie down and chew what has been received. Green pastures are not just for grazing—they are places for lying down. The love and mercy of God is not only in his gracious giving of rich pastures, but in the fact that he also makes me lie down when I have gathered enough.

We who live in an affluent society will do well to consider this insight from the twenty-third psalm. For most of us in America, the pastures have been green. We've been pretty good at foraging, gathering even more than we need. But often we have forgotten to lie down, to relax, to trust, to think, to enjoy, to grow. There is a time for gathering, but we cannot gather all the time. There must be a time for chewing the cud spiritually and mentally. There must be a time for soaking up the strength we have received; a time for digesting and making use of the insights and research we have accomplished.

Most of us have been good at gathering the abundance around us, but too few of us have been good at assimilating and enjoying our abundance. The man who is making enough money, yet works seven days a week and will not take time to worship, to play, to contemplate—this person will come to the time when God will make him lie down, even in the midst of green pastures.

If we are not content with what we can gather in a regular working week and insist on working, not only on our time, but on God's time, we soon get life out of balance. In a cow we call it bloat. Just what to call it in man is a problem, but we see it around us on all sides—in lives that have lost their meaning and direction; in homes that have become second-rate boardinghouses; in lives of boredom seeking escape through speeding, drinking, gambling, and other perversions of what are basically wholesome and normal drives in life. Sometimes it takes sickness, or mental breakdown, or some other upset to make us lie down, but if we will not do it ourselves, sooner or later we will do it anyway.

God restores my soul and my body, and the way he does it is to make me lie down even when the pastures around me are still green, even when others around me are still gathering. When I have had enough, he makes me lie down to use what I have and to be restored.

In the process of restoring, or healing, it is important for us to remember that it is God who does it. We are all blessed by progress in medicine and in the techniques of hospital care. But it is a fact that in actual healing no progress has been made at all. Medicine can improve the circumstances and make conditions more favorable for healing. The actual healing is something that we cannot control. We can guard against infection that will delay healing; we can put broken bones in line so that when they heal they will heal properly; but it is still God who heals. And he does it by making us lie down, by making us change pace—making us pause in the hurry of life so that the healing can take place.

When a weary body rests we call it sleep. When a weary mind relaxes we call it recreation. When worn-out soil is given a chance to grow grass and stop erosion and build up its fertility we call it conservation. When a weary spirit, worried about wrongdoings and stained by guilt, finds forgiveness and a new start in life, we call it salvation. And God is the one who does the renewing.

We troubled, hurried humans could learn a lot about spiritual growth from the humble cattle that know enough to lie down in green pastures. We need to learn to come to the end of the day and lie down in simple trust, knowing we have gathered enough for one day; knowing that it is time to just lean back on the goodness of God and trust that tomorrow there will still be plenty of time for more gathering. Most of us go through the green pastures of life too fast to really appreciate all that God has done for us. We need to take more time for chewing the cud.

When the Signs Have Been Destroyed

A few years ago I was hunting elk in a very rugged section of the Salmon River wilderness, an area where the creeks run down to the Salmon River through deep canyons and the north slopes are heavily timbered. We call this country the Salmon River "breaks" because it is the place where the high central Idaho plateau breaks away into a wild series of timbered slopes, rock slides, canyons, and crags; falling in a course of about twenty miles from an elevation of nine thousand feet to about three thousand feet at the level of the river in the bottom of the main Salmon River Canyon. Country like this is hard to travel in; it is easy to get lost in. But on this bright October day

WHEN THE SIGNS HAVE BEEN DESTROYED

I had no fear of getting lost. I was working my way along a well-blazed forest trail. I knew the trail led into the camp a few miles away where I had planned to meet my hunting partners. I was unfamiliar with the trail, but it was on my map and I knew that if it forked there would be a sign to show which way I should go. The U. S. Forest Service has done some excellent work in marking trails in the backcountry.

I had been taking my time and enjoying my hunting when I realized that the sun had dropped behind the mountains; I would have to hike right along if I would get into camp before dark. But I wasn't worried. It was a good trail, the sort that isn't too bad to follow even after dark. So I swung along the path, thinking of the stew the fellows would have cooking when I arrived and that cup of coffee that tastes so good on a crisp autumn night after a long walk in the mountains. I rounded a bend, walked into a thick patch of lodgepole pine, and there it was—not just a fork in the trail, but another trail intersecting the one I was following. I had three choices, and at first glance one looked as good as the other. I hesitated only a moment, then looked for the sign I knew would be there. And it was. A fine little metal sign showing to which creek drainage each trail would lead. But some vandal had come along ahead of me and had used the sign as a target for his big game rifle. There was not a chance of reading it. It was bent out of shape, and the enamel finish on it had shattered until the legend was gone.

When you depend on a sign to show you the way to get safely into camp before dark, it gives you a sinking feeling to find that the sign has been destroyed. For awhile I gave in to a feeling of anger. It is a disgusting and wicked thing for people to destroy signs that are needed by others. But I soon realized that it would take more than anger to get me into camp. I had three choices. One would take me to camp and a tent and a warm bed. The other two would mean a cold night out in the woods without a sleeping bag, no supper and no breakfast. A night out in the woods is not a serious matter if one doesn't lose his head, but it's not pleasant, and you know your friends will worry and wonder if you are hurt and unable to travel.

The destroyed sign gave me a feeling of desolation at first. Then I began to use my head a bit. The first man through that country had no signs and he found his way. How did he do it? The answer was clear. He found his way by following directions that are much more fundamental and much more enduring than any man-made signs. He worked out his own directions and trusted his own judgment.

With this in mind I climbed a little ridge where I could see over the thick stand of lodgepole. In the

WHEN THE SIGNS HAVE BEEN DESTROYED

remaining light of a quickly ending day I checked the way the water was running in the little canyon below me; I checked the direction of the sunset and I could see in the distance a peak I knew was part of the divide between the Salmon River and the Bitterroot River in Montana. I checked the distant landscape to see the natural passes through the hills, passes that the intersecting trail would likely lead to. Following this guidance I chose the right trail and shortly after dark arrived in camp to find the stew and the coffee even better than I had hoped for. I had found my way safely home, guided by things that no man had made, things that no man can destroy.

Often when I have faced a difficult decision or had a chance to help some friend with a difficult problem, I have thought of that nice little sign up there in the hills. It was a good sign, and the man who put it there wanted to be helpful. Surely it was a bad thing for a thoughtless hunter to destroy the sign, and it is possible that its destruction could cause someone to become hopelessly lost. But the sign was destroyed. And if one would travel with safety and pleasure in the backcountry, he would do well to learn how to find his way even when the signs have been destroyed. That little sign is a symbol of our time—a time when on every hand signs are being destroyed.

Small-town customs and close family ties that used to guide many people safely along the trail of life have been destroyed by our urban way of life with its impersonal organizations. Moral platitudes that guided many have fallen into disrepair. Even some of the great signs, like the Commandments, are being twisted or rewritten in language that makes it hard to see just which way they point in the confusion of a world that is changing so fast, we cannot keep up with all the new ideas, no matter how hard we try. What then shall we do? Shall we be angry with those who have destroyed the signs? We can if we like, but being angry will not get us safely into camp! There is a better way. And if we will look around us we can find our way by following directions that are much more dependable than the man-made signs. We can see which way the water flows, which way the sun sets. We can locate the evening star, and if the night is dark, perhaps the polestar itself.

In my own life I have found three basic landmarks that have guided me when it seemed to me the signs were destroyed or that some joker had twisted them around so they pointed in the wrong directions. The three things that I speak of are love, work, and faith. In the rough mountain country where I like to hunt we find our directions mostly by the way the water runs. Water never runs uphill, and many many times

I have found my way safely by following the course of a stream. A little stream will never go backward, it will never go around in a complete circle, and it will never deceive you. Many times in life when I have been very confused, I have found I could safely follow the way that was indicated by my love for my family, my friend, or my God. "Love never fails." I have known some very dark nights when I wondered which way I should go. But on the darkest night I have found that I could safely follow the direction indicated by the simple love that I have for my family and that my family has for me.

Work is another landmark that seems always to guide me in the right direction. When it seems that life is without purpose, when I am discouraged and confused, I find that some simple, creative task helps put me on the right path again; a task as simple as fixing a fence or pruning a tree or writing a letter. Work seems to be a fundamental signpost that cannot be destroyed by vandals, and when one knows the joy of a job well done he understands why the psalmist said: "Let the favor of the Lord our God be upon us . . . yea, the work of our hands establish thou it."

Along with love and work is faith for finding the right path when the signs are destroyed. Faith is like the North Star itself, for the darker the night, the brighter it shines. And no matter how confused one may be about the trail just ahead of his feet, he is never really lost as long as he has a star to tell him which way is north. Man-made signs are a good thing and a great convenience. But in a wilderness where signs can be destroyed, it is important to learn how to find your way home following directions that are not man-made and following landmarks that man cannot destroy.

Yellow Bells

"Why are you anxious . . . ? Consider the lilies of the field." Matthew 6:28

Just outside the gate at Sky Range Ranch there is a place on the hillside where the soil is very poor. This is range land that receives only ten or eleven inches of moisture a year. In the fall when the cows are coming home from the hills, they gather outside the gate, waiting to be turned into the pasture, and as a result this area has suffered severe overgrazing. On this poor ground plagued with drought and too many cattle, the plants are fighting a battle of survival. Since cows do not eat sagebrush, this hardy plant is holding its own pretty well. In the shelter of each clump of sage, little bunches of perennial grass cling to life, waiting to expand their holdings the moment they get their chance. And in the spring right after the snow melts, in this most unpromising soil, the yellow bells bloom. There will be about a week when the ground will be liberally sprinkled with these lovely little bells, each one on a stem about four inches high, swinging as gaily and bravely as if it had the whole world under control; as if drought and hungry range cows were no problem at all.

One year in March when the winter was very cold and spring was slow in coming, I walked over this area. The ground was still frozen; there was not a sign of life anywhere. I wondered: "Where are the yellow bells? Could it be that this is the winter when they died?" Then came a few warm days in April, and right behind the melting snow came the yellow bells, as delicate, as lovely, as brave as ever. When my daughter went through her annual spring ritual of bringing in a handful of yellow bells for the dining table centerpiece, I had some long thoughts. What a miracle is seen in this wonderful little flower. It does not give up, when the odds against it are extreme. It not only stays alive, but in its few short days of blooming it puts its energy into the production of beauty as well as life.

All of us need to look from time to time at the yellow bell or some other of God's lovely little things and reflect on what these little things have to say to us. Pain, hunger, frustration, death, loneliness, despair—these things have been always with us in this life. People have always felt hurried, always realized that life is too short for the things we long to do. To the people of Palestine two thousand years ago, the prospect of being run-through with a Roman spear was certainly as gruesome as our present fear of being disintegrated by an atom bomb. It was more likely! The prospect of growing old and begging alms was certainly as bad as the prospect of retiring with nothing but Social Security.

To these troubled people Jesus said: "Be not anxious. Consider the lilies of the field. Take a good look at them. Remember God cares for them. Surely you can trust him to do as much for you. And all your worry will not help a bit." We moderns of course have an added problem. Most of us do not get out in the field and we do not see the lilies or yellow bells at all.

Some friends were talking of their travels and found that each had been in California. As they compared notes, one asked: "What did you think of the redwood trees?" His friend replied, "What redwood trees?" After being shown on a map the location of the Redwood Forest, his comment was: "That must have been the day we made eight hundred miles." Surely here is a problem that we all face—the problem of going through a lovely world and missing it because we have set goals so big and so far away that all our time and energy is used racing toward the goals we may never reach.

There was once a time, around my sophomore year, when I thought graduating from college would be the greatest thing in life. Now, looking back, I cannot clearly remember the day I graduated. I cannot remember the commencement address or who gave it. But I clearly remember when I was a boy working on the hot afternoons weeding sugar beets and hiding from time to time under the large green leaves. I knew if no one saw me lie down, no one would know just where in the field I was. Under the beet leaves the ground was cool and damp. The hot sun was shut out, and there was a sense of privacy, a sense of being somehow very close to the earth and to God who made the earth. This lovely little place of my childhood I shall not forget. You may call it second childhood if you like. Thomas Bailey Aldrich speaks of a similar rare moment:

> My mind lets go a thousand things,
> Like dates of wars and deaths of kings,
> And yet recalls the very hour—

YELLOW BELLS

'Twas noon by yonder village tower,
And on the last blue noon in May
The wind came briskly up this way,
Crisping the brook beside the road;
Then, pausing here, set down its load
Of pine-scents, and shook listlessly
Two petals from that wild-rose tree.

As we go through life each of us is making a notebook of memories, whether we put our notes on paper or only on the pages of the mind. As we write, it is important that we note down some little things each day for that time when those notes may be our highest joy. So note the day the lilacs bloomed, the day your little son picked a dandelion for you, the day the bluebirds found the house you made for them. In this age of bigness, the big things will crush us if we forget to see the yellow bells, if we forget the words of one who said to consider the lilies of the field, and be not anxious.

A Guide or a Map

The Primitive Area of Idaho is a vast region of forests, mountains, lakes, and streams. In a wild symphony of crags and canyons this country pitches and breaks like some fantastic ocean of rock that suddenly was frozen at the moment of its most violent storm. In this wild sea of peaks and valleys the elevation varies from two thousand feet to ten thousand feet—mighty waves where one can often spend a full day climbing from the trough to the crest.

Because this country is so rugged that roads have never been built into it, it is called primitive, and the present-day traveler uses the same primitive form of transportation that was used by the Sheep Eater Indians a thousand years ago. Today we have improved methods of road building and it might be possible to build a road into some of this rugged country, but present-day administrative policy can see the value of a land that is unspoiled by modern means of travel; over two million acres of Idaho have been classified as Primitive Area, which means that roads will not be built into it.

The wildness and strangeness of this land is a part of its attraction; it has a mystery about it as well as natural beauty. There is a certain fascination about going into a country where few men have been, finding a remote spot for your camp, and thinking, with good reason, that perhaps no man has ever camped in this place before.

When I first moved to the Salmon River country I was eager for a trip into the wilderness. I had a good friend who was a forest ranger in a certain area that I wanted to visit. So at my first opportunity I went to him and asked if he had a detailed map of the area, a map I could use in making a trip through that part of the wilderness I wanted to visit. My friend told me he was sorry that he did not have a map as detailed as I wished for. But he said that in a few days he was going to make an inspection tour of the district and I would be welcome to ride along. Nothing could have pleased me more, and I made plans and took the trip with him.

It was a wonderful trip that I will long remember. We traveled through country where the breathtaking beauty was more than I had dared to hope for. We found mountain lakes where the trout fishing surpassed my fondest dreams. And through all this wonderful trip I never once worried about getting lost. My friend knew the way and I trusted him. I never had to study the map and worry lest I make a mistake, misread the map, and go in the wrong direction.

Many times since coming home from that wonderful trip I have had reason to remember it, and I have written in my little wisdom book the following comment: When taking a trip into a strange and unknown land, a guide is much better than a map. Many times when I have faced the problem of the death of a friend or loved one or have considered the fact that I too must face death one day, I have remembered this great experience. I think that in it there is a clue to our Christian faith concerning death and eternal life.

When we face death we know we face a journey into a strange land. No one has returned to give us the details concerning that country to which we go. Much as we long for assurance, we face the fact that we do not have a map to show us the way. But our faith does assure us that even though we do not have a map, we have a guide, a guide we can trust, a guide who is concerned about our welfare. And so we face the strange country called death with the assurance that God is the guide; God knows the way, and even in the valley of the shadow we have nothing to fear. He is with us, and he will guide us through the valley and out onto the green hill that lies beyond the valley.

I have found great comfort in the assurance that God is the guide and in the knowledge that a guide is better than a map. I do not need to know the way if I know the guide, and I do not need to know what the future holds if I know who holds the future. Death is indeed a mystery, a wilderness where I have not traveled before. But I believe it will turn out to be a wonderful wilderness surpassing even my fondest dreams.

> What no eye has seen, nor ear heard,
> nor the heart of man conceived, . . .
> God has prepared for those who love him.
> (I Corinthians 2:9.)

Death is a mystery, but it is a friendly mystery. When I was a child, Christmas morning was always a mystery. I never knew when I went to sleep what I would find when I woke up in the morning. But I always went to sleep with joy and excitement, for

I knew my father loved me, and knowing of his love, I knew that whatever I found in the morning would be wonderful and good for me. I could trust myself to the mystery because of my father's love.

One time I had to cross a strange river at night. In the darkness I could not see the other shore and I approached the crossing with fear. Then the man who ran the boat that was to take me across spoke to me, and at once I knew him as a trusted friend, a man who knew the river, a man whose ability I respected. My fear vanished. I did not need to know the way across the river if I trusted the one who was to take me across. So I crossed the dark river, and when I reached the other side I knew that my fear of the crossing was foolish; with a trusted guide there was nothing at all to fear. A guide is always better than a map.

With Wings like Eagles

There is a fascination in the flight of an eagle. Two pairs of eagles nest near Sky Range Ranch, and their hunting area is the drainage of Withington Creek, which runs through Sky Range. We have spent many pleasant moments watching these eagles making long, lazy circles in the sky. We try to imagine what the eagles are thinking about. Are they hunting or resting or just having fun? For it must be fun to be able to float in the sky, and floating is just what they do. I have watched for a long time without seeing the slightest indication of a wingbeat. The birds are simply riding the air currents, the thermal updrafts, and if you didn't know about updrafts of air, you would proclaim the flight of the big birds to be a miracle in defiance of gravity. No eye can see the power that keeps the eagle in the sky. But the eagle has learned to take advantage of this unseen flow of rising air that will lift him higher and higher without any effort on his part.

As I have watched the eagles, I have often thought it would be wonderful to have a power that could lift a person up and up, above his troubles and heartache, his shortsightedness and small-mindedness, to where he could just view the whole world and know he could stay above it and have no fear of it. Then I have remembered that we humans do have such a power to sustain us and lift us above our fears. It is the power of God and it can lift up those who trust in him.

The rising warm air will not hold an eagle up unless the eagle spreads his wings and launches out in faith, trusting the power of the thermal updraft. And the power of God cannot sustain us unless in humble trust we cast ourselves upon his mercy and trust in his goodness. Men and women of faith have found this power of God's love to be just as real for them as the air currents are for the eagle. I can imagine that a frightened, self-conscious eagle, putting more emphasis on his doubt than on his faith, afraid to believe and keep his wings spread, might have a bad time of it. He might even crash to earth and then say that his fall to earth "proved" that his doubt was correct and there really is no sustaining power.

When people are having a bad time with problems of faith, it often becomes evident that they have been frightened and unwilling to spread their wings. They have been self-conscious rather than God-conscious; they have been fluttering instead of flying. God has not promised us an easy life, but he has offered us an exciting, challenging life and power to sustain us in our need. The prophet Isaiah spoke of this great power to people who were defeated, discouraged, and having a hard and bitter life—a life much more difficult than most of us will ever see. He said:

They that wait upon the Lord shall renew their strength,
    they shall mount up with wings like eagles,
they shall run and not be weary,
    they shall walk and not faint.

I particularly like that part about walking and not fainting. When things are exciting or there is a crisis and I have to run, it seems that I manage pretty well. It is in the daily grind, the Monday-to-Friday walking and plodding, that I like to think about the eagles.

The Price of Potatoes

My first real lesson in economics came when I was twelve. It was in the year that the Great Depression of the early thirties started. Our neighbor had raised a fine crop of Idaho potatoes. Potato prices were good that winter. He had 5,000 hundred-pound sacks of U. S. No. 1 Idaho potatoes in his cellar. The buyer had offered him $4.85 a sack for them, and this added up to more money than the man had originally paid for his farm. As he visited with my parents, over the coffee cups I heard him gaily proclaim: "I'm holding them for $5." He also spoke freely of all the things he would be able to do with the money.

The "crash" came before he sold that potato crop.

THE PRICE OF POTATOES

Instead of selling them for $5 a sack he hauled them out and spread them on his hay fields for fertilizer. But they were very good potatoes, and they did not rot as rapidly as he thought they would. When he was mowing hay that summer the potatoes would catch on the points of his cutter bar and cause the mower to clog. He would have to stop the mower and get off and clean it. Clear over in the field where I was mowing I could hear him cursing his hard luck and reliving his bad experience. It got so bad for awhile that we worried about his sanity. He pitied himself so much for so long that he very nearly destroyed himself.

Since owning Sky Range Ranch, I too have known the disappointment that comes with unstable prices. It is hard to take disappointment. You have a good summer. The calves are some of the best you've ever raised. Then you take them to the auction when the market is bad. You come home with a check much smaller than you hoped for. There is not quite enough "to make the payment," a phrase familiar to all who live with a mortgage. You explain to the family that there will not be much for Christmas this year. The anticipated trip to Grandmother's will have to be postponed another year. Yesterday your plans were big and you were on top of the world. Today your plans have all but disappeared and your dreams have evaporated.

Sigmund Freud was never able to describe frustration more dramatically than did Lewis Carroll in his classic, *Alice in Wonderland*. Most of us remember Alice. She looks through a tiny door and sees an enticing garden, a place of heart's desire. But she is much too big to get through the door. Then she finds an answer to her problem—a magic drink that makes her grow small. She grows so small she can get through the door, but the door is locked, the key is on the table, and now she is much too small to reach the key. Then wonder of wonders, she finds something that will make her large. She grows large enough to reach the key, but alas, what good will it do? Now, of course, she is too big for the door. Utter frustration! So what does she do? She does what most people do when they are completely frustrated—she weeps. In fact, she weeps so much that she produces a pool of tears, and then when she grows small again she is in very real danger of drowning in the tears.

Alice, of course, is everyone. For everyone who really lives will find times when life is extremely frustrating; times when one feels so sorry for himself that he will just simply sit down and cry. And tears can be a blessing. Much of the sorrow of life is washed away by the soothing salt bath of tears. But tears can also be dangerous. Many lives are lost, as far as worthwhile living is concerned, by being drowned in the tears of self-pity.

Troubles are a part of life. They are given to us to help us grow. We are to use them to build on, not to brood on. And when we begin to feel sorry for ourselves, we are in real danger—danger of crying big, as Alice did, and then finding that our doing is so small and our crying so big, we are likely to drown in our own tears.

No marriage has ever been damaged by the tears of real sorrow. In fact, tears of this kind have a strange ability to bind two hearts together. But countless marriages have been washed out by the tears of self-pity. Useless remorse over past mistakes, crying over spilled milk is devastating. This is what happened to Lot's wife (Genesis 19:26). This couple found that they must move to a new home, but she kept looking back. I imagine she gave Lot a bad time. "If we had only stayed in Sodom. Why did this have to happen to us? Everything there was so fine—hot and cold running water, carpets on the floor, interesting neighbors." She kept looking back, and the scripture says she turned into a pillar of salt. I have always thought that salt was just the deposit which was left when the tears of self-pity evaporated!

Many tears are shed because we blame ourselves too much for something that happened. Or worse yet, we blame someone else. I know a woman whose little child was killed in a strange accident. It was no one's fault, but this woman brooded and blamed herself. She continued this until she almost lost her mind, her husband, and her home. This pool of tears is dangerous. Christianity teaches us that there are many things that happen in life that hurt and yet no one is to blame for them. They are a part of this world. In this world there is tribulation. But our challenge is to overcome the world.

It is interesting that Alice was saved from the pool of tears because she became concerned about the plight of the mouse that was also caught in the pool. As she sought ways to reassure the mouse, she suddenly discovered she was out of the pool herself. What an insight into life! The tears of self-pity can drown us, but we will never drown in the tears that we shed for another.

Joseph, the one we remember for his coat of many colors, surely could have been destroyed by self-pity. He was his father's favorite son. He could expect to inherit the home ranch. He "had it made." Then his wicked brothers sold him into slavery in Egypt. If he had been inclined to self-pity we would never have heard of him. But he was not this sort of person. And years later when his brothers asked forgiveness and were afraid of his power over them, he said: "You meant evil against me; but God meant it for good."

To be able to see in the worst that happens a stepping-stone to something greater in life; to take the worst that life can give and say, "God meant it to me for good"; here is the power to put self-pity in its place. What a sad fate it is to have our weeping so big and our courage so small that, like Alice, we face the danger of drowning in our own tears. What a sad thing it is to live in a world of beauty, surrounded with love and friendship, and then to fall into a pool of tears because of the price of potatoes!

The Grass Is Greener

In cattle country, where the cattle graze on the open range, the fence around a ranch is used as much to keep cattle out as to keep them in. At Sky Range Ranch, in the summer the cattle are out in the hills around the ranch and the grass on the ranch is saved for fall grazing. So in late summer the grass outside the ranch is grazed more than the grass inside the ranch, and the line fence makes a sharp contrast on the hillside.

I well remember the afternoon when my son and I had been riding the range checking on the cattle. We were nearing home in the lovely time of day when the setting sun casts long shadows and puts a halo on the hills; the time of day that can make a common sagebrush become a burning bush. About a mile from the ranch we had stopped our horses for a rest and we were just sitting, looking at the scene before us. Our line fence across the valley stood out sharply, like a giant pencil line on a great piece of green paper, and the sunlight accentuated the fact that the grass inside the ranch fence was much taller, richer, and greener than the grass outside where the cattle had been grazing all summer. Taking a long look at the scene, my son said: "Gee, Dad, look! The grass sure is a lot greener on our side of the fence."

Many times since that day I have paused to remember those simple words of a boy who could see what was set before him without being affected by the pessimism that sometimes comes with the passing of the years. For in life the grass is greener on our side of the fence. It is tragic that many people have subscribed to the old lie that says it is greener on the other side.

I think most of us have known times when we have been tired and discouraged, when we have compared our work with the work of some neighbor and have been tempted to say the grass is greener on his side of the fence. But when I start to give serious thought to jumping the fence, I am brought up short by the simple fact that on my side of the fence, though there are many problems, I also know something about the answers. I have faced the problems, started work on them, and if I jump the fence to go to what looks like greener pastures I will be trading a set of problems I know something about for a whole set of problems I know almost nothing about. The more I consider the situation, the more I realize that this is my side of the fence, and for me the grass is greener here.

We become weary of our daily work when we forget to savor each moment as a precious thing in itself. We forget that the meaning of life is in the present moment. We think that we will realize ourselves someday in some great achievement; that somewhere over the rainbow skies are blue. We think it will be great when our ship comes in. When we are single we work till we are married; when we get married we work till the children come; when the children come we work till they are raised; when they are raised we work till we can retire; and so on, until we find we have lived life and lost it. For the meaning of life is not in some great event someday, beyond some far horizon. It is right now. It is this very moment, which is like a silver coin in your pocket. You can put your hand on it and know it is good to have it there. This very moment you can work with God and serve him in your work and know the richness of his presence, and know what Jesus meant when he said the kingdom of

God is within you. It is time for us to realize that the kingdom is not coming. It is here, and we have either accepted it or rejected it; we have either entered it or stayed outside.

Much sorrow in marriage could be avoided if we would just remember that the grass is indeed greener on our side. One of the scandals of our present-day culture is the number of people who, when problems come up in their marriage, decide that the grass is greener on the other side of the fence. I do not know of a marriage that does not have some problems—at least two, a man and a woman. If there are children there are more problems. A marriage is a partnership, and almost any lawyer will tell you that a partnership is the most unsatisfactory and dangerous way of doing business.

If there were any way to manage a marriage without a partnership, I would be all for it. But there isn't. You can't run it as an individual enterprise and you certainly can't make it into a corporation. Whenever a problem comes up there is always a split decision, and there is no chairman to cast a deciding vote. The vote is always one to one, and this is why it takes real Christian grace to achieve a great marriage.

But the reward can be as great as the challenge. And whenever we seek to solve our problems by jumping the fence and heading for what looks like greener pastures, we deceive ourselves. The problems have a way of jumping with us. What looked like better pastures on the other side will turn out to be an illusion caused by the fact that we could not see clearly from our side that the other side had just as many burrs and weeds. What looked like greener pastures can turn out to be crabgrass.

Generally when people try to solve marriage problems by jumping the fence they simply trade known problems for unknown ones; and they have to face the new problems with the added burden of grief and guilt that comes from knowing they ran away from something that they should have faced up to and solved with the help of God—and perhaps a good marriage counselor. It is so much better to simply kiss and make up; to walk hand in hand in the evening up to some high place on the hill where you can see not only the house and yard, but the place where the creek runs through the big meadow, the place the birds come back to first in the spring, the woods in the back forty, and in the distance the everlasting hills. It is so much better to walk together to a place where you can get a better point of view and see that indeed the grass is greener on your side of the fence.

It is a wonderful thing when we learn that the grass is greener on our side of the fence. When we put away childish things and childish ways; stop crying for the moon and start counting our blessings. Even in these amazing days of space travel it is likely that most of us will never go to the moon. If we do, I think we will find that by contrast the old earth is not such a bad place after all. We can improve it a bit, if only in the place where we live, but we had better learn to thank God for it and appreciate it at least until he sees fit to put us in a better world than this.

Pessimism is a denial of faith. It is a way of saying we don't really believe the promises of God or appreciate his gifts. The mark of a Christian is optimism. Not a blind optimism that calls darkness light or denies that there is sin in the world, not an optimism that does not see the needs of the hungry or stops its ears to the weeping of those who suffer, but an optimism that knows that underneath are the everlasting arms. An optimism that says: "If God is for us, who is against us?"; an optimism that knows that in the world there is tribulation, but also knows the One who has overcome the world. And this optimism can spill over into every part of life and help us see that the grass is greener on our side of the fence.

Small Talk

A few years ago I attended an important national conference. There were many fine speeches by brilliant men and I was inspired and challenged. I returned home and a few days later left on a hunting trip with some friends. On this trip there was time for that highlight of big game hunting—the long evenings when you sit by the campfire and share your thoughts and feelings on a very intimate level. For me, I know, there was nothing I heard at the national conference that was as important in terms of giving my life real meaning as what was said by that campfire. My friend opened his heart to me and I could open my heart to him. This kind of talk is small, like a diamond, and very precious.

As I grow older and my time on this earth with my fellowmen grows shorter, I am sure that the high point of communication is not one man talking to millions in some great broadcast—it is one man talking to one man, heart to heart, mind to mind. It is possible to be so concerned with great speeches that we miss the meaning of great speech; we become so concerned with human relationships that we have no time for relationships with humans.

Many of us are so interested in big things—things too big to comprehend and much too big to achieve—that we lose our ability to possess lovely little things, things that could be ours for the taking. We are so interested in great talks between great men that we forget to have meaningful little conversations with ordinary folks like ourselves. A father is so interested in the comments of some world-famous commentator that he does not hear the comment of his own child about something he could share with his child. Summit talks have their place, of course, but our lives are desperately in need of talks on lower levels—face-to-face talks, sincere talks in the living room, dining room, and bedroom. It is easy for us to have our eyes and ears so fixed on big unions, big business, big bureaus, big explosions, that we do not see or hear the little sights and sounds that make life a pleasure and can save us from despair.

I have a poor memory, and as I look back over life there is much that I have forgotten. Certainly much that I learned in college and seminary has been forgotten, though it was presented to me as being very important. Most of the great speeches I have heard I have forgotten. But I am thankful that I have not forgotten the first time I found the nest of the redwing blackbird.

I was just a boy, and I rejoiced in the music of these birds as they mated and nested in the cattails along the drain ditch by our farm. Then I found that neatly woven nest of grass and horsehair and the pale blue eggs with the black lines and dots. I remember how I marveled that a bird could be so clever, and to this day I marvel for there is a mystery here that comes close to the mystery of life.

If one knew the mystery of the bird's ability to weave the nest of his kind without ever being taught, the mystery of the homing instinct of the migrating waterfowl, the mystery of the salmon returning to its spawning ground a thousand miles from sea, he would know the mystery of life itself. But he does not need to understand it; it is enough to perceive it and be blessed by it. It is enough to know that the mystery of creation is in a bird's egg, in a newborn calf, in a little creek that winds its way from the glacier on the mountain to the vastness of the sea, or in the little girl playing hopscotch on the sidewalk. How great is the poverty of those who do not see and talk about these little things.

How fortunate it is for most of us that the true riches of life are in little common things and we do not need to be famous or rich to find happiness. If greatness were necessary for happiness, of course, very few of us could ever hope to attain it. But God in his wisdom has put true happiness not in greatness but in smallness, so it can be attained by anyone who will seek and find, knock and enter. The little things that bring happiness are scattered all through life just as the wild flowers are scattered all over our springtime hills.

Just a few of these lovely things: the smile of someone who loves and trusts you; the beauty of a mother bird's care of her little ones; new grass coming up on a bare hillside; the fragrance of supper cooking when you are really hungry; the fascinating energy of an ant taking home some treasure five times as large as it is; the joy of making something with your own hands; the first words of a little child; a tomato from your own garden. Of course, the list is endless.

After an evening of small talk with a great friend, an evening when we have watched together the flaming logs of our fire turn to glowing embers, I have often thought of the wise words of the great Englishman Samuel Johnson. Boswell discusses with Johnson the matter of keeping a diary but confesses to Johnson that he is afraid he will put into his diary too many little incidents. Johnson replies: "There is nothing, sir, too little for so little a creature as man. It is by studying little things that we attain the great art of having as little misery and as much happiness as possible."

Like a Shepherd

"He will feed his flock like a shepherd,
  he will gather the lambs in his arms,
he will carry them in his bosom,
  and gently lead those that are with young."
                            Isaiah 40:11

I have a fine saddle horse named Nellis. She is rather high-strung, and temperamental, and has some very definite likes and dislikes about people. In fact, she is so temperamental that I have to be careful who rides her lest someone should get bucked off. The horse is well trained, and I think she resents people who ride her as if she were a pack mule. My eldest daughter, Heather, is very fond of Nellis, and because of the mutual regard involved Heather seems to be the favorite with Nellis. I am sure Nellis likes Heather better than she likes me. And one who has never seen the affection that a girl can have for a horse has missed something very beautiful.

A few years ago Nellis was frightened by something, probably a bolt of lightning or a bear, and jumped into a barbed wire fence. She was about a mile from our house up on a grassy hillside where she often grazed. It was Heather who first found her—weak from loss of blood, stiff and crippled from the deep, nasty wire cuts in her front legs. With tears of compassion streaming down her cheeks, Heather spent two hours leading the injured horse down the hill and into the barnyard. I don't think I could have done it. I doubt if the horse would have followed anyone less sensitive to her suffering. The pain in those crippled legs must have been intense, especially while Nellis was getting down the steep part of the trail. When I came home that evening and saw the horse I felt sure she would never run again; never again would she and Heather proudly bring home a ribbon from the horse show.

But I underestimated my daughter's care of the horse. Every morning and every night for several months, regardless of weather and other activities,

Heather devoted herself to the needs of Nellis. She disinfected, washed, and anointed with oil—soothing oil, healing oil. Nellis runs now as well as she ever did, and I will never again read the words "thou anointest my head with oil" without seeing in my mind a crippled, suffering horse and a little teen-age girl; a girl who day after day was up at daylight or before and out the door in rain, snow, or sub-zero weather because she cared. Our God is like that!

When I was a boy I lived on a farm. I worked hard and played hard and walked a mile to school. I carried a sack lunch to school to eat at noon and by the time school was out at four o'clock I was always hungry. By the time I walked home I considered myself starved. To this day I can still remember the smell that would hit me when I opened the door on the days that my mother baked bread. How eagerly I reached out for the large piece she would have ready for me. I think there were some nights I would have sold my birthright for that slice of bread. And sometimes I wonder, do we really know what we are reading when we read those words: "I am the bread of life; he who comes to me shall not hunger"? After that dash home from school on a crisp autumn afternoon, nothing could have meant more to me than my mother standing there in the kitchen with that wonderful homemade bread. Our God is like that!

I'm sentimental and my children mean a lot to me. When one of my children comes running to me with a skinned knee, I drop whatever I am doing and do what I can to heal the hurt with ointment, perhaps a band-aid for the knee, and a handkerchief to wipe away the tears. I know a strange and wonderful joy when I am able to comfort my children. Do we remember that God is like that? "God . . . will wipe away every tear from their eyes, and death shall be no more, neither shall there be mourning nor crying nor pain." What I do is on a very human level. But I am glad that Jesus used this very human example of the father-child relationship to tell us what our Heavenly Father is like. We need to sense the reality of this.

I think back now and understand better than I did then some of the things that my parents did to care for me during the bleak days of the Great Depression. And I remember God is like that. "What man of you, if his son asks him for a loaf, will give him a stone? Or if he asks for a fish, will give him a serpent? If you then, who are evil, know how to give good gifts to your children, how much more will your Father who is in heaven give good things to those who ask him?"

Sometimes I think I am too sentimental. I remember how I had to blink back the tears while I roped a little filly and tied her down and pulled some horrid porcupine quills from her tender nose. She cried and whimpered. I could not make her understand why my concern for her caused me to hurt her so. Sometimes our God is like that—his love for us is why he has to hurt us. And we cannot understand it at all.

I remember a little orphan heifer we raised. She didn't seem to have the same herd instinct that the other cows had, and the first year I turned her out on the range, when fall came, she and her calf did not come in with the other cattle. For parts of two days I rode hard, covering the steepest and most isolated parts of our range, always fearing I would find her dead. Then one evening my phone rang. It was my neighbor saying he had seen my cow and her calf in a little isolated canyon where she had settled down for awhile, perhaps not knowing for sure which way to go to get home. There was a joy I felt at this news, a joy that goes far beyond the matter of mere economic loss or gain. At daylight the next morning I rode out to bring her home.

What rancher has not had this experience that makes so real the meaning of the great passage that says, "If a man has a hundred sheep, and one of them has gone astray, does he not leave the ninety-nine on the hills and go in search of the one that went astray?" Our God is like that. He is like that, only infinitely more so.